My Science Library

# Let's Investigate Light

## by Buffy Silverman

## Science Content Editor:
## Shirley Duke

Rourke
Educational Media

rourkeeducationalmedia.com

*Teacher Notes available at*
rem4teachers.com

Science Content Editor: Shirley Duke holds a bachelor's degree in biology and a master's degree in education from Austin College in Sherman, Texas. She taught science in Texas at all levels for twenty-five years before starting to write for children. Her science books include *You Can't Wear These Genes, Infections, Infestations, and Diseases, Enterprise STEM, Forces and Motion at Work, Environmental Disasters,* and *Gases.* She continues writing science books and also works as a science content editor.

www.rourkeeducationalmedia.com

Photo credits: Cover © Suto Norbert Zsolt, Baevskiy Dmitry, Fesus Robert; Pages 2/3 © Vlue; Pages 4/5 © Vaclav Volrab, Andrea Danti; Pages 6/7 © sebikus, silver tiger, Sailorr; Pages 8/9 © WebStudio24h, Christian Lopetz; Pages 10/11 © Vlue, My Portfolio, grynold, Merlinul, Ruslan Grechka, Mara008, martan, maple, MANSUROVA YULIA, Pedro Nogueira; Pages 12/13 © Christian Lopetz, prochasson frederic; Pages 14/15 © Nejron Photo, SasPartout; Pages 16/17 © takayuki, Chiyacat; Pages 18/19 © Adam Gilchrist, Alila Sao Mai, Sandra van der Steen; Pages 20/21 © HeinSchlebusch, jolly

Editor: Kelli Hicks

*My Science Library* series produced by Blue Door Publishing, Florida for Rourke Educational Media.

**Library of Congress PCN Data**

Silverman, Buffy.
 Let's Investigate Light / Buffy Silverman.
    p. cm. -- (My Science Library)
 ISBN 978-1-61810-108-2 (Hard cover) (alk. paper)
 ISBN 978-1-61810-241-6 (Soft cover)
 Library of Congress Control Number: 2012930306

Rourke Educational Media
Printed in the United States of America,
North Mankato, Minnesota

**rourkeeducationalmedia.com**

customerservice@rourkeeducationalmedia.com
PO Box 643328  Vero Beach, Florida 32964

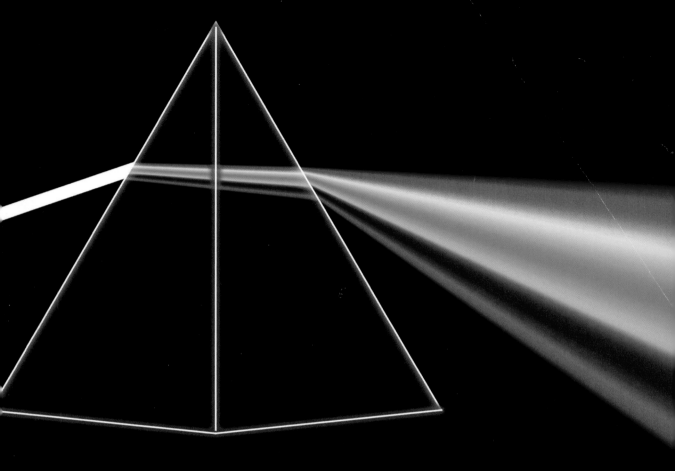

# Table of Contents

# We Need Light

When you plant seeds in a garden, green plants sprout. Sunlight shines on new plants, and they grow roots, stems, and leaves. After flowers open, they are pollinated and grow into fruits. You harvest tomatoes, corn, cucumbers, beans, and blueberries. How do plants get energy that they need to grow these structures?

Green plants get their energy from sunlight. They can use this energy to make food through a process called **photosynthesis**. All other living things depend on plants or animals that eat plants for energy.

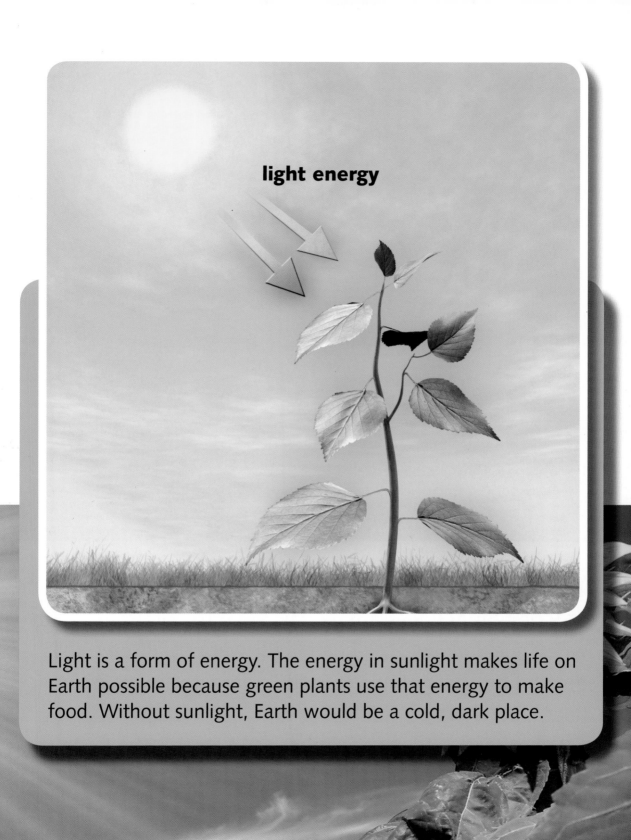

**light energy**

Light is a form of energy. The energy in sunlight makes life on Earth possible because green plants use that energy to make food. Without sunlight, Earth would be a cold, dark place.

Sun

For most of human history, people had only sunlight and fire for light and warmth. Today, we turn on electric lights when it is dark and use heaters for warmth. But we still depend on sunlight as the Earth's ultimate source of light, heat, and energy.

What makes light and darkness on Earth? The Earth spins on its **axis** as it travels around the Sun. As it spins, the side facing towards the Sun has daylight. Night falls on the side turning away from the Sun.

It is always dark somewhere on Earth. At night we can see light from the stars and reflected sunlight from the Moon. Many stars are bigger than the Sun, but they appear less bright because they are much farther away from Earth.

**Moon**

Earth

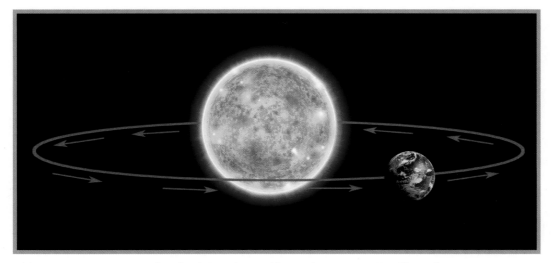

*You experience daylight when the place on Earth where you live faces towards the Sun. Twelve hours later that spot faces away from the Sun, and you experience night. The Earth rotates around its axis every 24 hours and orbits the Sun in one year.*

# Light Travels

For thousands of years people have wondered how light reached Earth. Many early scientists thought rays of light traveled in straight lines. Later, scientists believed that light traveled as tiny particles. In 1801, an English physicist named Thomas Young showed that light traveled in waves. Imagine a wave of water rolling up and down. Young discovered that light energy travels in the same motion.

*On a sunny day you see beams of light shining through the gaps in tree branches.*

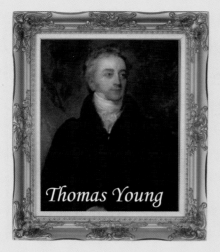
Thomas Young

Thomas Young designed an experiment to show how light traveled. He made two slits in a card, and then shone a beam of light through the slits and onto a screen. If light traveled as particles, he expected to see two bright lines on the screen. Instead he saw bands of light and dark. He concluded that two waves of light traveled through the slits and interfered with each other, making the dark bands. If you make two sets of ripples in water, the waves will overlap and interfere with each other in a similar manner.

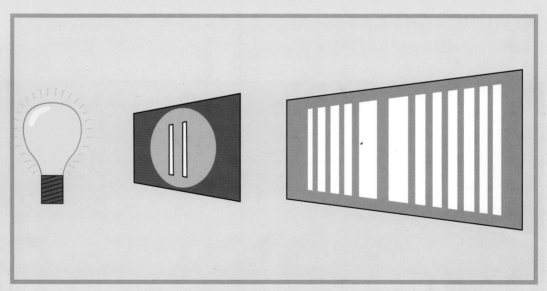

*Shine a light through a card with two slits to reproduce Thomas Young's experiment. Can you show that light travels in waves?*

Once scientists understood that light moves in waves, they thought differently about light. Waves have special properties, including size which is measured as **wavelength**. A wavelength is the distance from the peak of one wave to the peak of the next.

When white light shines through a prism, the prism bends the light and separates it into a rainbow, called the **visible spectrum**. Each of the seven colors that make up the spectrum has a different wavelength.

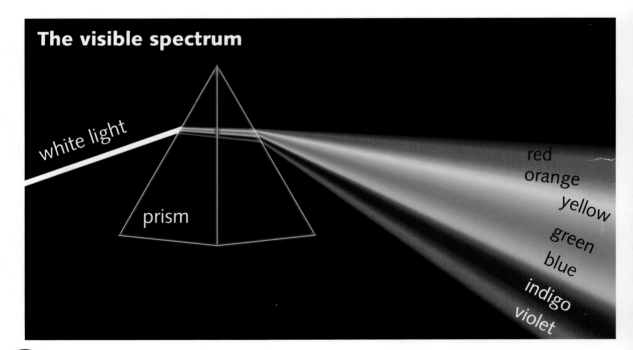

The visible spectrum

white light

prism

red
orange
yellow
green
blue
indigo
violet

*James Clerk Maxwell*

In 1864, James Clerk Maxwell showed that light was made of an electric and a magnetic field. Electric waves and magnetic waves are linked together to form lightwaves, which are also called electromagnetic waves.

People can see light with wavelengths between 390 and 750 nanometers (a nanometer is one-billionth of a meter). This range of light is called the visible spectrum. Infrared waves, radio waves, and microwaves have longer wavelengths. **Ultraviolet**, x-rays, and gamma rays have shorter wavelengths.

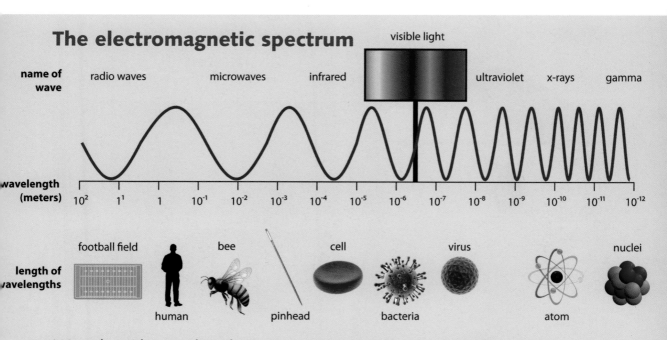

## The electromagnetic spectrum

*Wavelengths on the electromagnetic spectrum range from very short gamma rays to radio waves which are close to the size of a football field.*

Another important property of a lightwave is its **frequency**. The frequency of a lightwave is the number of waves that pass by a certain distance in one second. If more waves pass by in a given period of time, the light has more energy. Frequency is also related to wavelength. Short waves have high frequencies, and long waves have low frequency.

*The waves in this chart have the same frequency.*

*The waves in this chart have different frequencies.*

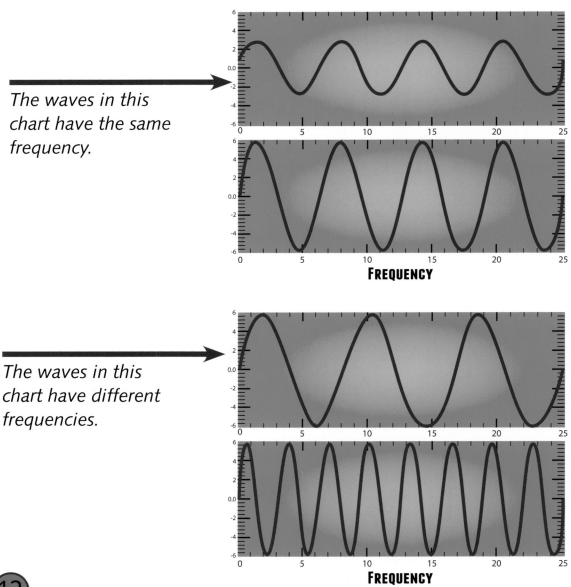

Some animals see parts of the spectrum that are invisible to people. People cannot detect high frequency ultraviolet light, but bees can see it. Many flowers that bees pollinate have patterns visible only in ultraviolet light. The photograph below shows how a flower appears to a bee.

**How this flower looks to a human.**

**How this flower looks to a bee.**

Even after it was known that light moves in waves, some scientists still wondered if light was also made of particles. Albert Einstein concluded that light is made of streams of tiny particles, called **photons**, which move in waves. Photons carry energy.

Light can travel through space, where there is no **matter**. Solids, liquids, and gases are all made of matter. When lightwaves collide with matter, they transfer energy to it. Sunlight feels warm because the energy of light is transferred to your skin.

*When you're at the beach your skin is exposed to light waves from the Sun. Light waves also reflect off water and sand and reach your skin. Sunscreen protects your skin by scattering and reflecting light waves.*

# Speeding light

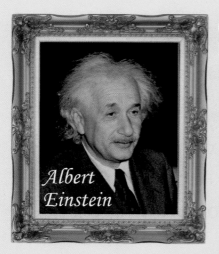

*Albert Einstein*

In 1905, Albert Einstein calculated the speed of light in space as 186,282 miles per second (299,792 kilometers/second). According to Einstein, the speed of light is the fastest that energy and matter can travel.

Solar panels are used to make electricity. When the Sun shines on solar panels, photons from light are absorbed by solar cells. The energy is transferred to the solar cells, causing electricity to flow.

# Properties of Light

To see an object, light must **reflect** off of it and travel to your eyes. Light bounces off rough surfaces and scatters in all directions. When lightwaves hit a flat, shiny surface, they are reflected back with the same pattern.

*When you stand in front of a mirror light bounces from your body, to the mirror, and back at you. Light bounces off the mirror at the same angle that it strikes the mirror. If you move to the right, your reflection appears to move to the left.*

*The images of trees and boats are reflected off the smooth surface of water.*

As light travels through different materials, its speed changes. Light slows when it moves from air to water and from water to solids. This changing speed makes light bend and change direction and is called **refraction**.

*You can see light bending by placing a straw in a glass filled with water. The straw appears broken where water meets air.*

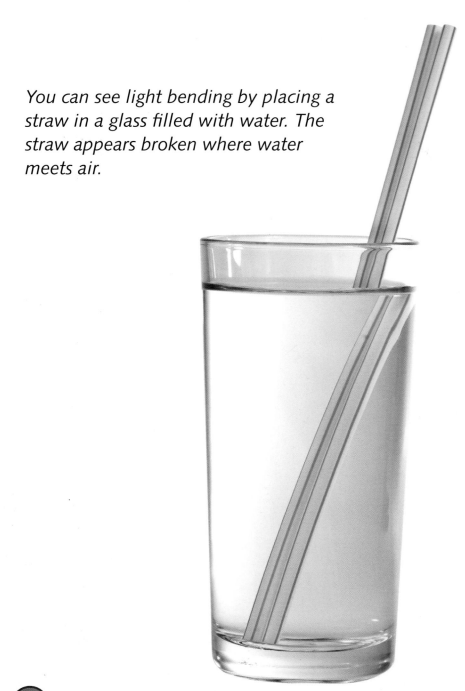

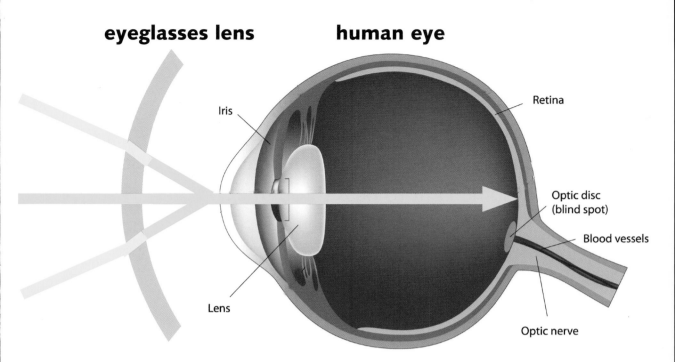

## eyeglasses lens          human eye

Iris

Retina

Optic disc
(blind spot)

Blood vessels

Lens

Optic nerve

*When light passes through eyeglasses, the curve of the lenses bends lightwaves. Glasses focus an image on the retina, the part of the eye that reacts to light, and sends information through the optic nerve to the brain.*

*Lenses in cameras, microscopes, telescopes, and glasses are shaped to bend light. Different lenses make objects appear near or far.*

19

Light travels through some materials and not others. You can see light pass through a clear window. Clear materials that let light pass without being reflected are called **transparent**. **Translucent** materials like cloth allow only some light to pass through and reflect some of it so the light is scattered. **Opaque** materials do not let any light through; they absorb or reflect all of the light.

*Light passes through the glass windows, but not through the walls or window frames.*

*Stand outside on a sunny day. Your body is opaque, it blocks light-waves, and a dark shadow forms on the ground. Lightwaves travel in a straight line, and cannot bend around you.*

Are you ready to experiment with light? Try this! Does a glass of water make a shadow? Compare that with the shadows made by tree leaves and branches. See what else you can discover when you investigate light.

# Show What You Know

1. What causes light to bend?

2. How is the frequency of lightwaves related to energy?

3. Why do you see your image in a mirror?

# Glossary

**axis** (AK-siss): an imaginary line running through the middle of the Earth, around which it spins

**frequency** (FREE-kwuhn-see): the number of light waves that pass a certain point in a certain time period

**matter** (MAT-ur): anything that has mass and takes up space

**opaque** (oh-PAKE): not letting light pass through

**photons** (FO-tans): units of light energy

**photosynthesis** (foh-toh-SIN-thuh-siss): the process by which plants use light energy to change water and carbon dioxide into food

**reflect** (ri-FLEKT): to bounce off an object, as a lightwave

**refraction** (ri-FRAK-shun): change in direction of a lightwave when it travels from one medium to another

**translucent** (transs-LOO-suhnt): substance that allows some light to pass through, but not all light

**transparent** (trans-PAIR-uhnt): clear substance that lets light through so objects can be seen on the other side

**ultraviolet** (uhl-truh-VYE-uh-lit): light that cannot be seen by the human eye, and has shorter wavelength and higher frequency than visible light

**visible spectrum** (VIZ-uh-buhl SPEK-trum): range of lightwaves that can be seen by people

**wavelength** (WAYV-length): distance between two peaks in a wave of light or sound

# Index

## Websites to Visit

http://micro.magnet.fsu.edu/optics/lightandcolor/primary.html

http://missionscience.nasa.gov/ems/09_visiblelight.html

http://www.neok12.com/Light-Optics.htm

## About the Author

Buffy Silverman loves to spend summer days at Lake Michigan, watching sunlight dance on the water. When she's not enjoying the great outdoors, she writes about science and nature.

Ask The Author!
www.rem4students.com